D1278178

URANUS

by Ruth Owen

WINDMILL
BOOKS

New York

Published in 2014 by Windmill Books, An Imprint of Rosen Publishing
29 East 21st Street, New York, NY 10010

Produced for Windmill by Ruby Tuesday Books Ltd
Editor for Ruby Tuesday Books Ltd: Mark J. Sachner
US Editor: Joshua Shadowens
Designer: Tammy West
Consultant: Kevin Yates, Fellow of the Royal Astronomical Society

Photo Credits:
Cover, 1, 10–11, 13, 16 (bottom), 17 (center), 20–21, 22–23, 24, 26–27, 28–29 © NASA;
4–5, 6–7 © Superstock; 8–9, 12, 14–15, 16–17, 18–19 © Shutterstock; 14–15 (center)
© Ruby Tuesday Books; 19 © Public Domain; 25 © Science Photo Library.

Library of Congress Cataloging-in-Publication Data

Owen, Ruth, 1967–
 Uranus / by Ruth Owen.
     pages cm. — (Explore outer space)
 Includes index.
 ISBN 978-1-61533-728-6 (library binding) — ISBN 978-1-61533-773-6 (pbk.) —
 ISBN 978-1-61533-774-3
 1. Uranus (Planet)—Juvenile literature. 2. Voyager Project—Juvenile literature. I. Title. II. Series:
Owen, Ruth, 1967– Explore outer space.
 QB681.O935 2014
 523.47—dc23
                                        2013014721

Manufactured in the United States of America

CPSIA Compliance Information: Batch # BS13WM: For Further Information contact Windmill Books, New York, New York at 1-866-478-0556

CONTENTS

URANUS, THE ICE GIANT

Uranus is the seventh **planet** from the Sun in our **solar system**. It is a huge, cold world that **orbits** the Sun at an average distance of 1.7 billion miles (2.7 billion km).

Mercury, Venus, Mars, Jupiter, and Saturn, which are the five planets nearest to Earth, can be observed with the naked eye. The earliest humans would have seen these planets in the night sky. **Astronomers** did not know Uranus existed, however, until telescopes became available.

Today, we know that huge, distant Uranus is blue because of the amount of methane gas in its **atmosphere**. We also know it has many **moons** and a system of dark, icy rings encircling it. There are many mysteries still to be unraveled, however, because unlike the planets closer to Earth, Uranus is difficult to see, even with the most powerful telescopes. Also, unlike planets such as Venus or Mars that have been visited by spacecraft and robots, only one spacecraft, NASA'S *Voyager 2*, has ever visited this faraway planet.

That's Out of This World!

Both Uranus and Earth are orbiting the Sun.
Uranus is many millions of miles (km) from our home
planet, however. The closest the two planets
ever come together during their orbits is about
1.6 billion miles (2.6 billion km).

This is an artist's impression of Uranus. Along with Neptune, Uranus is known as an ice giant.

THE BIRTH OF A SOLAR SYSTEM

About five billion years ago, the Sun, Earth, Uranus, and everything else in the solar system did not exist.

The chemical ingredients to make the Sun, eight planets and their moons, **dwarf planets**, **asteroids**, and every other object in the solar system did exist, however. These ingredients were floating in space in a vast cloud of gas and dust.

Over millions of years, part of the cloud began to collapse on itself, forming a massive rotating sphere, or ball. Around the sphere, a spinning disk formed from the remaining gas and dust. The material in the sphere was pressed together by **gravity**, causing it to heat up and pressure to build. Eventually, the heat and pressure became so great that the sphere ignited. In that moment, a new star, our Sun, was born!

Gas and dust continued to spin in a disk around the Sun. Over time, material in the disk clumped together to form all the objects in the solar system. One of the objects that formed on the outer edges of the spinning disk was the planet Uranus.

That's Out of This World!

A vast space cloud where stars form is called a nebula. Nebulae are also known as "star factories" or "star nurseries." Nebulae are trillions of miles (km) wide and can be many different shapes and colors.

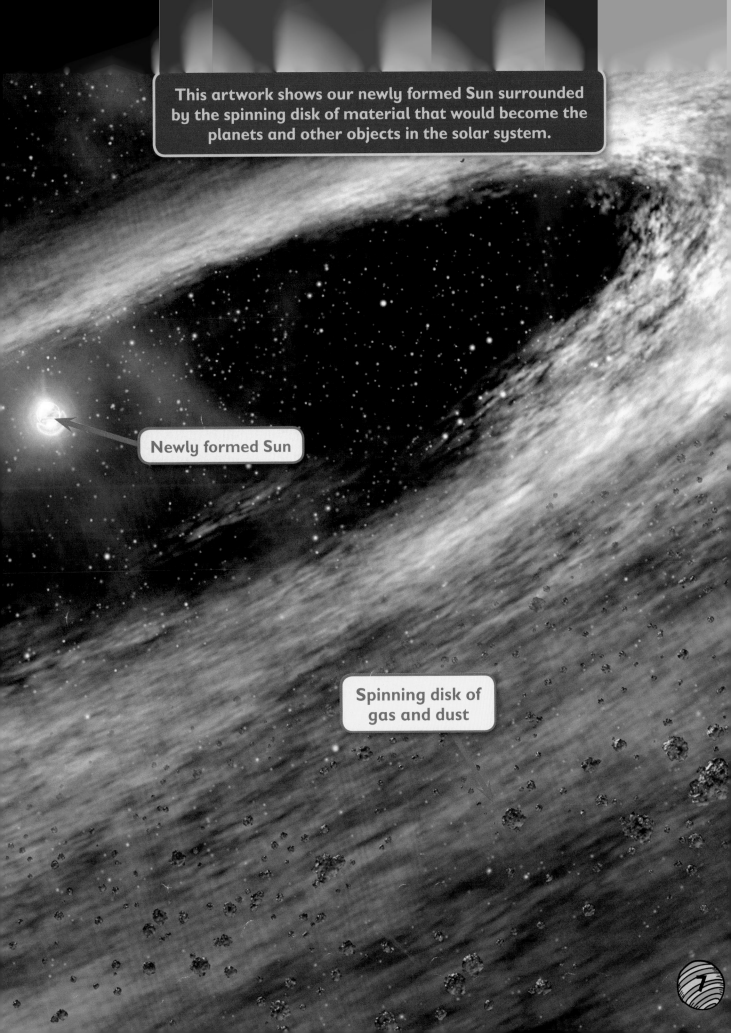

This artwork shows our newly formed Sun surrounded by the spinning disk of material that would become the planets and other objects in the solar system.

Newly formed Sun

Spinning disk of gas and dust

7

Imagining Our Solar System

The solar system is measured in billions of miles (km). It can be hard to imagine distances that are so vast. There is a fun way, however, to experience the scale of the solar system and visualize the size of the planets in comparison with each other.

If you take a bowling ball and imagine that it is the Sun, then small planets such as Mercury and Mars and the dwarf planet Pluto could be represented by pinheads. Venus and Earth would be the size of a peppercorn. Uranus and Neptune would be the size of a pea. Saturn would be marble-sized, and giant Jupiter would be the size of a chestnut.

In this scaled-down version of the solar system, tiny pinhead Mercury, the closest planet to the Sun, is 10 yards (9 m) from the bowling ball Sun. Earth would be 26 yards (24 m) from the Sun. Distant pea Uranus would be a massive 496 yards (454 m) from the Sun. Most amazingly, pinhead Pluto would be about the length of 10 football fields away from the bowling ball Sun!

A bowling ball =
the Sun

A pea = Uranus

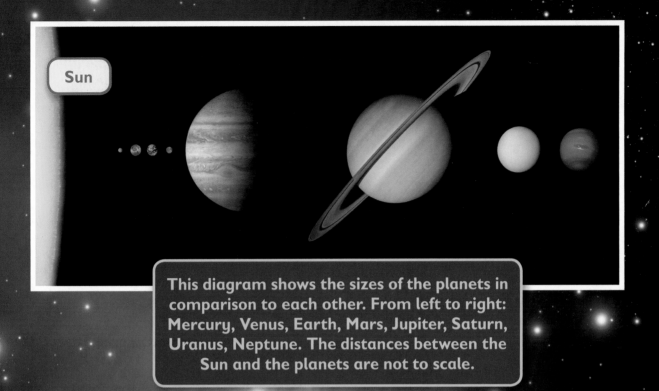

Sun

This diagram shows the sizes of the planets in comparison to each other. From left to right: Mercury, Venus, Earth, Mars, Jupiter, Saturn, Uranus, Neptune. The distances between the Sun and the planets are not to scale.

That's Out of This World!

The solar system's eight planets do not all have the same structure. The planets closest to the Sun, Mercury, Venus, Earth, and Mars formed with solid, rocky surfaces. The four furthest planets, Jupiter, Saturn, Uranus, and Neptune, do not have a solid surface. These planets are made mostly of gases and liquids.

URANUS'S DAYS AND YEARS

Like our Earth and the other planets and objects in the solar system, Uranus orbits the Sun. As it travels through space, it is moving at about 15,200 miles per hour (24,477 km/h).

The time period that it takes a planet to make one full orbit of the Sun is called a year. Earth orbits the Sun once every 365 days, so a year on Earth lasts for 365 days. Uranus is much farther from the Sun than Earth, however, so its journey takes longer. In fact, it takes Uranus 30,687 days to make one full orbit. So a year on Uranus actually lasts for 84 Earth years! During that long year, Uranus makes a journey of 11,201,335,967 miles (18,026,802,831 km).

As the planets in the solar system orbit the Sun, each one also rotates, or spins, on its **axis**. Earth rotates once every 24 hours. Uranus rotates faster than Earth, though, and makes one full rotation in just over 17 hours.

Pluto

That's Out of This World!

If you looked at Earth from above the North Pole, you would see that the planet is spinning counter-clockwise. Mercury, Mars, Saturn, Jupiter, and Neptune also spin in this direction. Uranus and Venus, however, spin in a clockwise direction.

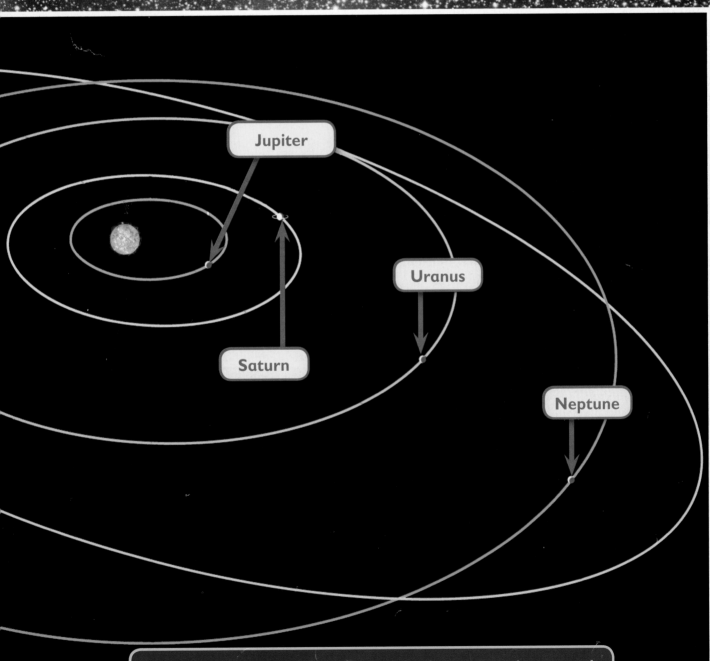

Jupiter

Uranus

Saturn

Neptune

This diagram shows the orbits of the four outer planets and the dwarf planet Pluto. The distances are not to scale.

THE SIDEWAYS-SPINNING PLANET

As a planet rotates on its axis, it could be described as spinning like a top.

The planets are slightly tilted, so each planet's axis is also at a slightly tilted angle. For example, Earth's axis is tilted at 23.5 degrees. Even with a slight tilt, most of the planets still rotate in a nearly upright way. Uranus, however, is so tilted on its axis that it is actually spinning on its side!

No one knows how Uranus came to be spinning so differently than all the other planets. The most popular theory, though, is that at some time, billions of years ago, Uranus was hit by another enormous space object. Before the collision, Uranus was spinning in an upright position, like Earth. The impact of the collision was so great, though, that it knocked Uranus onto its side, leaving it to become the sideways-spinning planet.

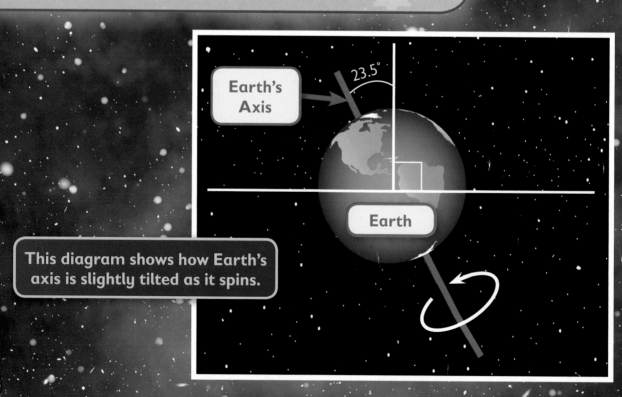

Earth's Axis

23.5°

Earth

This diagram shows how Earth's axis is slightly tilted as it spins.

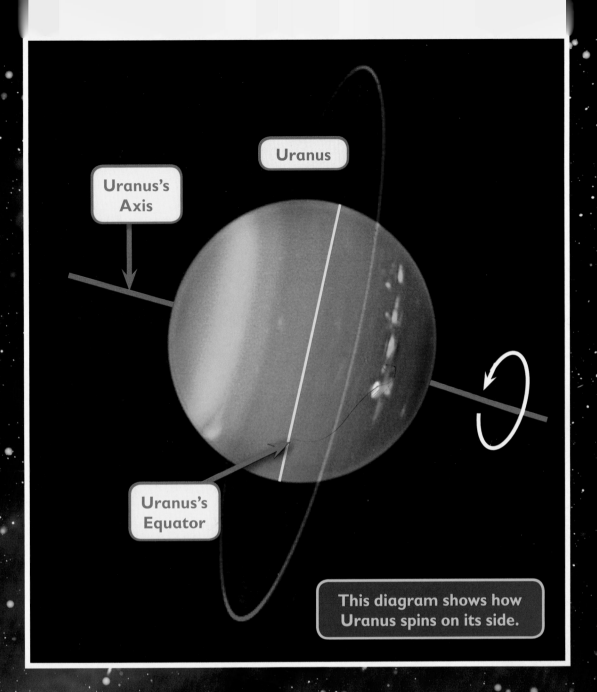

Uranus's Axis

Uranus

Uranus's Equator

This diagram shows how Uranus spins on its side.

That's Out of This World!

If you could drive a car at 60 miles per hour (97 km/h), day and night without stopping, it would take just over two weeks to drive around Earth's equator. To drive around Uranus's equator, however, would take nearly 10 weeks.

A 21-YEAR WINTER!

Just like the other planets in the solar system, Uranus has seasons, days, and nights. Each season on Uranus lasts for about 21 years, however, because it takes the planet 84 years to make one orbit of the Sun.

During one of Uranus's 21-year-long seasons, the equator faces the Sun, and the entire planet experiences autumn. As the planet moves through its orbit into winter, the north pole points away from the Sun, and the planet's northern **hemisphere** has about 21 years of winter. As the north experiences winter, the southern hemisphere has a long summer. During the next 21 years, the entire planet passes through its spring, and then the northern hemisphere experiences a 21-year summer, while the south has a long winter.

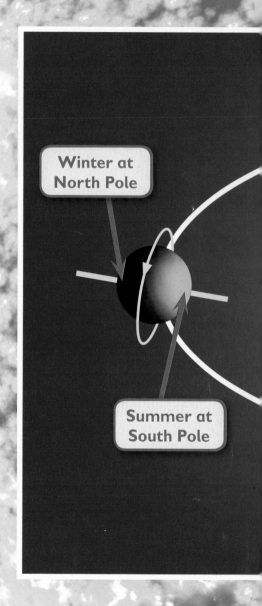

Winter at North Pole

Summer at South Pole

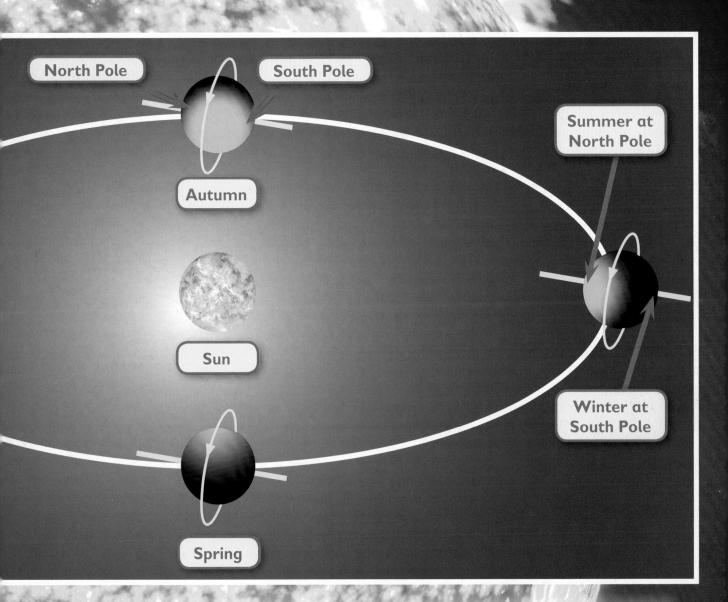

North Pole

South Pole

Summer at
North Pole

Autumn

Sun

Winter at
South Pole

Spring

That's Out of This World!

As Uranus's north or south pole points toward the Sun, that
hemisphere experiences daylight. In fact, it experiences
about 42 years of daylight, while the other hemisphere
is plunged into nearly 42 years of darkness!

URANUS, INSiDE AND OUT

As one of the gas giant planets, Uranus does not have a solid surface. It is a massive ball made mostly of gases and liquids.

Surrounding Uranus is an atmosphere that is made up mostly of hydrogen and helium. The atmosphere also contains a small amount of methane, water, and the gas ammonia. It is the methane in Uranus's atmosphere that gives the planet its blue color. As light from the Sun penetrates the planet's atmosphere, clouds beneath the atmosphere reflect the light back out. Light is made up of different colors, though, and the methane gas in the atmosphere absorbs the red parts of the light. It then allows only the blues and greens to be reflected, so we see Uranus as a blue-colored planet.

Beneath Uranus's atmosphere is a deep layer of icy liquids including water and liquid methane and ammonia. Deep inside the planet, scientists believe there is a solid core of rock.

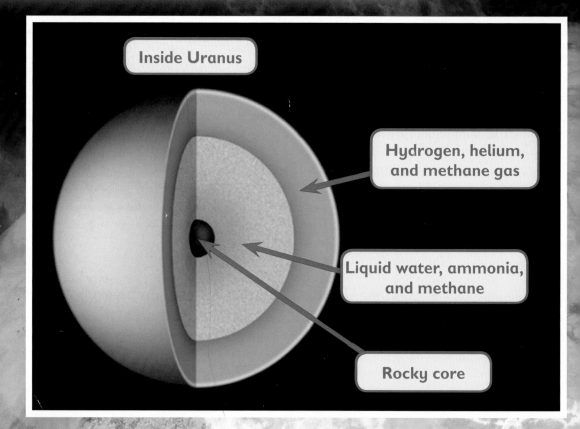

Inside Uranus

Hydrogen, helium, and methane gas

Liquid water, ammonia, and methane

Rocky core

16

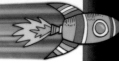

That's Out of This World!

Because Uranus is made up of gases, it is very light for its size and does not have as much gravitational pull as a heavy rocky planet like Earth. Uranus's gravity is about 86 percent of the gravity on Earth. This means if you weighed 100 pounds (45 kg) on Earth, you would only weigh 86 pounds (39 kg) on Uranus.

Earth
Radius = 3,959 miles
(6,371 km)

Uranus
Radius = 15,759 miles
(25,362 km)

The Sun
Radius = 432,169 miles
(695,509 km)

Discovering Uranus

Uranus was the first new planet to be discovered after the invention of the telescope in the early 1600s.

William Herschel was a German-born British astronomer who built his own telescopes. In March 1781, Herschel was studying space looking for stars. When he first observed Uranus, he believed it was a star or perhaps a comet.

Herschel was not the first astronomer to have seen Uranus. Others had viewed it through telescopes in the previous 100 years and had also believed it was a star. After further studies, Herschel was able to confirm that the object he'd first seen on March 13, 1781, was in fact a planet orbiting the Sun beyond the orbit of Saturn.

Herschel wanted to name his planet Georgian Sidus, which is Latin for the "Georgian Star," in honor of the British king at the time, George III. It was eventually named Uranus, however, after the Greek god of the sky.

That's Out of This World!

The Romans named the planets they could see in the sky after their gods Mercury, Venus, Mars, Jupiter, and Saturn. When astronomers discovered Uranus and Neptune centuries later, they continued to name them for ancient Roman or Greek gods.

William Herschel

This is a model of the telescope that William Herschel used to discover Uranus.

URANUS'S MOONS

A moon is a naturally occurring satellite that orbits a planet. Mercury has no moons, Earth has one, while Mars has two. Uranus has 27 known moons. There could still be more to be discovered, however!

Uranus's five largest moons were the first to be observed by astronomers using telescopes from here on Earth. In 1787, William Herschel discovered the planet's two largest moons, Titania and Oberon. Even though Titania is the planet's largest moon, it is still only half the size of our moon with a diameter of just 980 miles (1,578 km).

In 1851, British astronomer William Lassell discovered the moons Ariel and Umbriel. Nearly 100 years then passed before American astronomer Gerard Kuiper discovered Miranda, in 1948. For several decades, Uranus had only five known moons, and it would be 1986, when *Voyager 2* visited the planet, before more moons were discovered.

Umbriel

Ariel

Oberon

Titania

Uranus

Miranda

That's Out of This World!

Earth's moon is named *the Moon* because early astronomers did not realize that other moons existed. The moons of the other planets in the solar system have more glamorous names. Some of Uranus's moons are named for characters from Shakespeare's plays.

MOON SECRETS REVEALED

When NASA's *Voyager 2* spacecraft flew by Uranus in 1986, it discovered 10 more moons.

Since *Voyager 2*'s discoveries, another 12 small moons have been discovered using the Hubble Space Telescope. Today, we know of 27 moons orbiting Uranus. Finding these smaller moons has been difficult. They are nearly 2 billion miles (3 billion km) from Earth and have diameters as small as 10 miles (16 km). Scientists believe they could be asteroids that have been pulled into orbit around Uranus by the planet's gravity.

In addition to discovering new moons, *Voyager 2* and the Hubble Space Telescope have allowed us to see and find out more about the planet's largest moons. We know they are made of ice and rock. We know Oberon has a mountain that is 3.7 miles (6 km) high, and that Miranda has giant canyons that are 12 times as deep as the Grand Canyon!

That's Out of This World!

The Hubble Space Telescope orbits Earth outside of our atmosphere. Unlike telescopes on Earth, Hubble can detect distant objects in space more clearly because its view is not blurred by the gases in our atmosphere.

The Hubble Space Telescope orbiting above Earth

Titania

Miranda

Ariel

URANUS'S RINGS

Astronomers had been studying Uranus for nearly 200 years when the planet revealed the surprising secret that it has rings.

In 1977, two groups of astronomers were observing Uranus as it passed in front of a star. One team was at the Perth **Observatory** in Australia. The other team was aboard the Kuiper Airborne Observatory (KAO). The KAO was an aircraft fitted out to be a flying observatory that could fly 9 miles (14 km) above Earth's surface. At this height, there is less interference from clouds and the Earth's atmosphere, so astronomers are able to view space more clearly.

As the two teams of astronomers watched Uranus pass in front of the star, the star's light was blocked in an unexpected way. The objects causing the blockage of light were rings encircling the planet. Today, thanks to *Voyager 2*'s visit to Uranus in 1986 and observations by the Hubble Space Telescope, we know that Uranus has at least 13 rings encircling it.

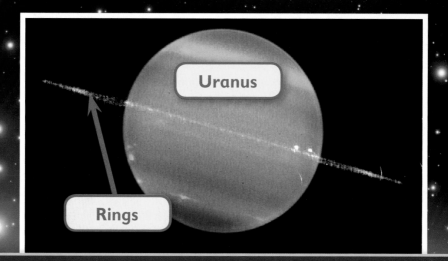

Uranus

Rings

This image of Uranus's rings was captured by equipment at W.M. Keck Observatory, which is on the summit of Mauna Kea in Hawaii.

Artwork showing the rings of dark, icy material surrounding Uranus

That's Out of This World!

Unlike Saturn's more famous icy, rocky rings that contain pieces of ice as large as mountains, Uranus's rings are made from chunks of material no bigger than 65 feet (20 m) wide.

VOYAGER 2

In 1977, NASA'S spacecraft *Voyager 1* and *Voyager 2* were launched on a mission to visit the solar system's outer planets.

The mission was possible because the orbits of the planets Jupiter, Saturn, Uranus, and Neptune were **aligned** in a way that only happens every 175 years. This rare alignment allowed the *Voyagers* to visit a planet and then use the gravity of that planet like a slingshot to propel them onto the next planet. Originally, the plan was that the two spacecraft would visit Jupiter and Saturn. The *Voyagers* functioned so successfully, however, that it became possible to extend their missions.

Voyager 2 launched from the Kennedy Space Center at Cape Canaveral, Florida, on August 20, 1977. *Voyager 1* actually launched after *Voyager 2* on September 5, 1977.

Voyager 2 reached Jupiter in July 1979 and Saturn in August 1981. After four years in space, the spacecraft's instruments were still functioning well, so it was sent on its way to Uranus.

That's Out of This World!

In case the *Voyagers* ever encounter an alien civilization, each spacecraft carries a gold-plated copper disk containing information about humans and Earth. The equipment to play the disks, like records, is also aboard the *Voyagers*. Each disk includes 115 pictures, Earth sounds, pieces of music, and greetings in 60 languages.

The disk carried by each *Voyager* spacecraft

Voyager 2 blasts off aboard a *Titan/Centaur* rocket on August 20, 1977.

GLOSSARY

aligned (uh-LYND)
Placed or arranged in a straight line.

asteroids (AS-teh-roydz) Rocky objects orbiting the Sun and ranging in size from a few feet (m) to hundreds of miles (km) in diameter.

astronomers (uh-STRAH-nuh-merz) Scientists who specialize in the study of outer space.

atmosphere (AT-muh-sfeer) The layer of gases surrounding a planet, moon, or star.

axis (AK-sus) An imaginary line about which a body, such as a planet, rotates.

dwarf planets (DWAHRF PLA-nets) Objects in space that have certain characteristics that distinguish them from other bodies orbiting the Sun. One of these is that the object be large enough and its gravity be strong enough to have caused it to become nearly round. Also, its orbit around the Sun cannot have been swept clear of other bodies, as would be the case with the larger planets, and it must not be a moon of a larger planet.

equator (ih-KWAY-tur) An imaginary line drawn around a planet that is an equal distance from the north and south poles.

gravity (GRA-vuh-tee) The force that causes objects to be attracted toward Earth's center or toward other physical bodies in space, such as stars, planets, and moons.

hemisphere (HEH-muh-sfeer) A half of a planet or other astronomical body, divided either into northern and southern halves by the equator or into eastern and western halves by an imaginary line passing through the north and south poles.

moons (MOONZ) Natural objects that orbit a planet.

nebula (NEH-byuh-luh) A massive cloud of dust and gas in outer space. Many nebulae are formed by the collapse of stars, releasing matter that may, over millions or billions of years, clump together to form new stars.

observatory (ub-ZUR-vuh-tor-ee) A structure or building that houses a telescope or other equipment for studying space.

orbits (OR-bits) To circle in a curved path around another object.

planet (PLA-net) An object in space that is of a certain size and that orbits, or circles, a star.

satellite (SA-tih-lyt) An object that orbits a planet. A satellite may be naturally occurring, such as a moon, or an artificial satellite used for transmitting television or cell phone signals.

solar system (SOH-ler SIS-tem) The Sun and everything that orbits around it, including asteroids, meteoroids, comets, and the planets and their moons.

WEBSITES

For web resources related to the subject of this book, go to: www.windmillbooks.com/weblinks and select this book's title.

READ MORE

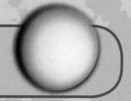

Loewen, Nancy. *The Sideways Planet: Uranus*. Amazing Science: Planets. Mankato, MN: Picture Window Books, 2008.

Roza, Greg. *Uranus: The Ice Planet*. Our Solar System. New York: Gareth Stevens Leveled Readers, 2010.

Slade, Suzanne. *A Look at Uranus*. Astronomy Now! New York: PowerKids Press, 2007.

INDEX